The Five Elements of Intimacy

by Gary M. Douglas and Dr. Dain Heer

AC PUBLISHING

The Five Elements of Intimacy

ISBN: 978-1-63493-761-0 (paperback)
ISBN: 978-1-63493-762-7 (ebook)

Published by Access Consciousness® Publishing
www.acpublishing.com

Table of Contents

Foreword

Welcome to a new way of looking at intimacy and relationships!

We learned about what we call "the five elements of intimacy" from our friend Mary, who was born in England in 1913. She was raised by her conservative British grandmother until she moved to New York City in the mid-1930s where she met her husband Bill. They moved to Santa Barbara when Bill retired.

Mary and Bill were together for over fifty years and they had one of the most intimate and caring relationships we've ever seen. The energy that flowed between them was beautiful.

Mary showed us that becoming intimate with your partner always begins with becoming intimate with yourself, and we watched as she continuously put the five elements of intimacy into practice in her life and her relationships.

The five elements that create great intimacy are honor, trust, allowance, vulnerability, and gratitude. Each of these elements offers a unique perspective of the creation of intimacy, with oneself or with others. Access Consciousness® aims to create oneness with all, and these five elements are the bases from where to start. Within these pages are tools, examples, exercises and questions to explore what true intimacy is like and what it takes to create it.

A Note to the Reader

Challenging your assumptions, conclusions, decisions, judgments, and expectations about people and relationships isn't easy, but if you wish to have truly intimate relationships, it's something you have to do. Here are a few tips for getting the most out of this book as you read:

- Be willing to be brutally honest with yourself.
- If you find yourself defending a point of view, holding onto a judgment, or trying to prove yourself right, pause and ask yourself, "Is it light? Or is it heavy?" When you do this, you will start knowing instantly when something is true for you, allowing you to choose accordingly.
- You can also ask, "Is what I'm doing in my relationship really working for me?" Notice whether your answer makes you feel lighter or heavier.

Intimacy is about joy! We encourage you to play with these elements and experiment. Ask questions about what can work for you. Try out the questions and exercises. Ask, "What else is possible here?"

Are You Ready to Start Creating Intimate Relationships?

The five elements of intimacy are honor, trust, allowance, vulnerability, and gratitude. Each one is essential if you wish to create truly intimate and fulfilling relationships. In the chapters that follow, we will talk about each one of these elements and how you can work with it to create more intimate, satisfying and enjoyable relationships.

Notice that sex is not included in the list of the five elements that create intimacy. Sex is about body parts getting intimate, but it's not about true intimacy. Sex does not create intimacy, although greater intimacy often creates greater sex. If you are looking for information about how to have greater sex, you might like to read our book *Sex is Not a Four-Letter Word, But Relationship Oftentimes Is.*

INTRODUCTION

A New Way of Looking at Intimacy and Relationships

True intimacy is created by trusting, being in allowance, not judging, honoring, and having gratitude. You must first have these elements with yourself before you can have them with another. What does this mean? It means you must include yourself in the equation of your relationship with others. It's about bringing yourself as you truly are—with all your quirks, preferences, interests, and ways of being—to create a truly intimate relationship. Because if you're not present as yourself in the relationship, how can it even be called a relationship?

If you're like most people we work with, one of the first things that happens when you start a relationship is that you think, "I can't tell him this thing about me because he'll think badly of me" or "I can't say this to her because she won't like me." You decide that the other person is going to judge some aspect of you, and because you don't want that to happen, you begin to divorce the parts of yourself that you judge. What's even more strange is that you will often begin the process of changing yourself to what you *think* they will like, even before you've chosen to meet for your first date.

Let's say you love to watch the news and talk about current events, but your new partner couldn't care less about that, so you stop watching the news. Or you eat meat and your girlfriend doesn't, so you change your eating habits to match hers, even if that doesn't work for you. Or you run marathons, and the other person thinks that is beyond boring, so you stop training, and in the process, you give up being yourself.

This is not going to create the kind of intimate relationship you want, yet we continuously see people do this with their partners, as well as with their kids, friends, and relatives. But how can you create intimacy with someone if you cut yourself off from the things you love and enjoy in life? The idea is not to turn yourself off in a relationship. It's to turn yourself on, along with everyone who is around you!

Have you ever gotten together with a new partner and started cutting out of your life the things and people you truly enjoy? Were you worried that the things you loved wouldn't fit with your new relationship? How much time did you spend trying to accommodate others' needs in your relationships while you lost yourself in the process? When in a relationship with another, you must be honest with yourself of who you are, what you value, enjoy doing and having in your life.

When you are not intimate with yourself, you project a lot of need onto other people. You begin to look to them to provide everything for you that you won't—or maybe believe you can't—provide for yourself. It becomes their sole responsibility to prove you're loveable, to acknowledge where you're great and to validate everything you choose, as though that will foster it in you. You catch yourself saying things like, "I need someone to love me. I need someone to see me and acknowledge me. I need someone to care for me and to value me." But when you're intimate with yourself, it's a completely different story. You lose your sense of doubt, and you value yourself in a different way. It allows you to acknowledge and care for yourself—as well as for the other person.

Creating a Divorceless Relationship

How much time have you spent trying to accommodate others' needs in your relationships while denying your desires and, therefore, losing yourself in the process?

What if each person in a relationship could be himself or herself and could choose to share that with their significant other? This is what we call a divorceless relationship, a relationship in which you don't have to divorce any part of yourself in order to be with someone else.

Here are some questions you can ask that will get you started on looking at how you may be divorcing yourself in your relationship. This is an essential first step in creating true intimacy with yourself and others.

- **Have I stopped doing some of my favorite things since I've been in my relationship?** Have you given up salsa dancing or listening to your favorite type of music? Have you stopped reading the books you love, or hiking, or going to the quirky ethnic restaurant you are crazy about? Have you adopted your partner's interests and hobbies and dropped your own? What would it be like if you were part of your partner's life and they were a part of yours?

- **Have I lost my connection with other people and things?**
  Have you stopped connecting with nature or old friends or family members?

- **Do I have the idea that I need to change in order to have a relationship?**
  What would happen if you let go of the idea that you need to change in order to have a relationship? How would it be if you began to recognize that you are pretty wonderful just the way you are right now?

- **Have I been excluding myself in my current or most recent relationship?**
  When you notice that you're separating, energetically or emotionally from yourself, and you make a demand of yourself to stop divorcing yourself, this behavior can begin to change. Realizing you are doing this is an important first step. This isn't about being harsh, unkind or judging yourself for having done it. To the contrary, it is about honoring yourself. You express your strong, clear intention to stop divorcing yourself and to be as incredible as you truly are with no ifs, ands, or buts. Honoring yourself is not a license to dishonor your partner. It doesn't

mean you have to leave the relationship or can't compromise for something that works for everyone.

What we would love to see is a different sort of conversation, where we all acknowledge that there is something fundamentally great about all of us and we ask, "How do we live as that greatness?"

The fact is that you are an infinite being with infinite awareness and choice, and as such, you have an innate capacity for intimacy with everyone and everything around you, without limits or barriers. Yet most of us have been taught innumerable ideologies that create separation and tell us that we are limited. We struggle with money. We wrestle with our relationships. We don't honor and believe in ourselves. But what if all the concepts we've been given about ourselves aren't true? What if we're not limited at all? What if we're miraculous—and that's the thing we are not willing to be? We suggest that you ask, "What if all the concepts I've been given about who I am or who I am supposed to be aren't true? What if I, as an infinite being, am capable of far more than I ever considered?"

An infinite being knows, perceives and receives infinitely. We all have the capacity to function in this way but most of us have been taught to operate from unconsciousness and anti-consciousness, and when we do that, our life and relationships become difficult. We have been taught to believe that we are limited and finite. Pause for a moment to look at that statement. What are some of the things you think you aren't capable of knowing, doing, or accomplishing? Then ask yourself, "Is that really true? Where did this idea come from?"

We are inviting you to become intimate with who you truly are and to create a genuinely intimate relationship with yourself, your partner and everyone and everything in your life.

You Have to Function from Your Awareness

Creating great intimacy with another person is not about learning a bunch of rules, methods, or techniques. It's about choosing to be aware. If you would like to have a truly intimate relationship, you have to function from your awareness. In an intimate relationship, this requires being in allowance of your partner's choices, ideas and desires without requiring you to agree or reject them. Awareness (or our definition of consciousness) is the ability to be present in your life for every moment without judgment of yourself or anyone else. It's the ability to receive everything, reject nothing, and create all that you desire in your life, greater than what you currently have and more than what you can imagine.

This is something that comes to you naturally. You have the inborn capacity to be aware of everyone and everything around you, and this awareness is essential in creating every part of your life. Awareness is not something you can think yourself into, it's simply something you have and are, but we've been taught you can only know what you've learned. This isn't so.

A lot of us have had parents, spouses and friends who have discouraged us from recognizing our innate capacity to be aware. They've told us things like, "You're wrong, you don't know that," or "You can't know that." They diminish your knowing by asking, "How do you know that?" instead of encouraging your innate capacity to just know that you know. Have you bought into that point of view as real and true and denied that you can actually know what is true for you? Here's more on the simple tool that can get you started on accessing your awareness of your infinite knowing:

Tool: Is It Light? Or Is It Heavy?

If something is true for you, the energy of it will feel light, nurturing, and spacious. There will be a sense that anything is possible. You may feel that your awareness has expanded and more choices are available to you. You have probably experienced this at some stage in your life. Have you ever been bogged down in a difficult situation or tried to resolve a seemingly impossible problem and suddenly realized what you needed to do? Can you recall how that felt? Did it feel lighter–more spacious? Feeling lighter is a sure sign that you are becoming aware of what is true for you and what will create.

If something isn't true for you, the energy will feel heavier, twisted, or dense. There will be a sense of finality or conclusion instead of a sense of space and possibility. No other choices will seem available. You will experience a sense of contraction and feeling small. Feeling heavy indicates there is a lie in place that you've either bought into or are trying to buy into as true for you. Recognize whatever it is as a lie, let it go, and ask more questions.

Following what feels lighter will assist you in navigating your life. Here are some questions to get you started:

- If I choose this, what will my future be like?
- If I don't choose this, what will my future be like?
- If I do this, what will my relationship be like afterward?
- Do I desire to continue to choose this person, event, or situation? Yes? No?

The light or heavy tool does not mean one thing is better than another. You are not choosing the right or wrong thing to do, as right and wrong requires judgment. Light or heavy is simply acknowledging the energy of the situation, the choices available and which direction will help you to create what you are asking for. How might your life and relationships begin to change if you weren't looking for the right or wrong choices? Can you imagine what that would be like? What if you stopped judging everything as right or wrong and instead started using light and heavy as your barometer?

We're inviting you to honor your awareness and to choose what feels light—to spend time with people, animals, books, or movies that make you feel light, and watch the changes that start to show up in your world.

Judgment Is the Antithesis of Awareness

If you are like most people, you have been taught to create judgments and come to conclusions about everything and everyone in your life, including yourself. We're suggesting that there is a totally different way of being with people and things: to be aware with total allowance. Allowance is not acceptance. Acceptance is you say you like them despite their flaws, which is nothing but judgment. Allowance is seeing all of them without judging any part of them as good or bad. It doesn't matter whether someone is being selfish and unkind or whether they are being gentle and generous. You simply perceive what they are doing without adding definitions, judgments or decisions to what you have perceived.

You may have bought into the idea that if you're aware of someone's limitations, you're judging them. But you may simply be perceiving how they are functioning without adding any meaning to it. That's what you want to go for. This is the key to understanding the difference between a perception and a judgment.

Every judgment you make is a nail in your coffin. Why is that? Because once you make a judgment like, "He is the perfect man for me," or "She will always be my best friend," you won't allow anything that doesn't match that judgment to come into your awareness. You trade your ability to be aware of a person as they are for the judgment you have made about them, and as a result, you are no longer able to see them and what they may be doing, even if they are trying to stab you in the back. It's the same with negative judgments. Once you decide that someone is an idiot, a fool, or whatever the judgment happens to be, you impede your ability to see anything beyond the judgment you have made. Judging someone limits both of you. If you judge them as an idiot, you cannot perceive when they are brilliant, they can't contribute fully and may cause them to doubt themselves. This creates less choice for everyone. When you can be aware of them fully without the filters of judgment, greater things become possible.

The antidote to judgment is awareness. When you are being truly aware, everything is included in your world, and nothing is judged or excluded. You see the good, the bad, the beautiful, and the ugly for what they are—not the way you *want* them to be, not what you *thought* they would be, not what they *ought* to be, but just for what they *are.*

Chapter 1

Honor

Honoring Yourself

The first element of intimacy is honor. Our friend Mary was a superb example of what honoring yourself looks like. She was a totally irrepressible and energetic woman with a hearty laugh and a wonderful sense of humor, who never paid a bit of attention to what other people might think of her or how they might judge her. She was who she was, and she didn't separate from herself. Mary had a large circle of friends who participated in a variety of interests including traveling. She wasn't stopped for a minute by her husband Bill's lack of interest in those things. Bill never tried to discourage her or complain about the money she was spending.

In honoring herself, Mary brought who she was to the relationship, and Bill did the same. She was intensely interested in metaphysics and spent her life doing metaphysical research. She turned her learning from classes and seminars into practical assistance with people facing limitations.

Bill worked as an advertising executive and believed you lived once then you died and became worm food. He couldn't have disagreed more with Mary's views, for example her ideas about reincarnation, but he honored her viewpoint. And she did the same with him. They didn't argue, they didn't make each other wrong, and they didn't try to change the other. Mary and Bill honored each other and themselves as well. It was extraordinary to see a couple doing that.

Sometimes Bill would invite Mary to join him and his advertising clients for cocktails and dinner. Mary would put on a conservative dress, little white gloves and a pillbox hat, and on the way into the restaurant, Bill would say, "Mary, please don't talk about metaphysical stuff with my clients," and she would always reply, "Of course, darling."

Honoring the Other Person

Mary said, "Bill took care of me. He did what was needed to make my life better, and I did what he needed to make his life better. When he asked me not to talk about the things I was interested in with his clients, I felt it was correct to honor him in the same way he honored me."

When you are honoring someone, you perceive without judgment what's going on for them in the moment. You see who they are and where they are functioning from. You recognize what they desire, what they can have, what they can't have, what they think is important, and what they don't think is important, and you honor and respect that.

Whatever the other person is choosing, you allow it to be what it is, and you permit it to change when and if it changes. You can question the other person in a way that allows them to make a different choice, but you don't push them in a direction you think they should take. If you are pushing them in a direction you think they should take, you are judging your point of view as the correct one. As you practice allowance of each other's choices, the honoring builds and creates a greater possibility of intimacy for both of you.

Know That the Leopard Isn't Going to Change Its Spots

During the early years of Gary's friendship with Mary, he was married to a woman who spent money as fast as he could make it, and she would often empty the bank accounts without telling him. This was difficult for Gary because he would write checks to pay the people who worked for him, but when they took the checks to the bank, there would not be enough money in the account to cover the checks and the bank would refuse to honor them.

Gary recognized there was no way in hell that his wife was going to change her financial behavior—no matter what he did, no matter what he said, no matter how much they talked about it—because she didn't want to change. She thought she did a great job of handling money. So, what did he do? He realized he could honor the fact that her financial behavior was her way of doing things. At the same time, he could honor himself, and the people who worked for him, by making sure he had enough money to cover his obligations. Gary started to set cash aside so he would have enough money on hand to cover his employees' pay.

Gary finally got to a point in their relationship where he realized that he was continuously divorcing parts of himself to make the marriage work. This is what most people do. They dishonor themselves, they divorce themselves, in order to create a relationship. Eventually, Gary decided to end the marriage, and in doing so, he did his best to honor his wife as well as himself. He made sure she got a substantial financial settlement because he wanted to honor the commitment he had made and give her a decent income. Gary wasn't mean; he wasn't ugly. He simply knew that he couldn't live with her anymore, and it was honoring himself, and honoring her, to handle the divorce in this way.

What Honors You?

When people first hear about intimacy, they think it means concession—that you would be willing to cut off your arms and your legs for a partner. But what it's actually about is honoring and caring for yourself as well as the other person.

If what honors you is going out and riding a horse, even if that's not what your partner does, then you're honoring yourself when you ride. You don't dishonor your partner by expecting them to take up horseback riding and they don't dishonor you by getting upset that you aren't spending all your time with them. If they love to watch football or read science fiction novels, or go to the gym, you don't dishonor them by trying to get them to do something you find more fun and interesting. You take care of yourself, you do what's right for you, and you honor your partner and trust that they will take care of themself.

What Does Dishonoring Your Partner Look Like?

Dishonoring your partner can take many forms. It can be expressed by a lack of regard for them, by not paying attention to them, by belittling them, or by not treating them with concern, respect or esteem.

A woman who was not happy in her marriage called her husband and told him that if he didn't change in the ways she had demanded, she would go off with another person. Her attitude was: "My husband isn't doing what I want him to do, so I'm going to control him by threatening to leave." She said, "I told him that because I wanted to be honest with him."

Saying that wasn't being honest, it was being mean and cruel. Threatening to leave in that manner was like a knife in the back. Why would you do that to someone you care about? Even if she was going to leave him, telling him what she said was not an honest or a kind thing to do. She was not treating him with regard. Regard would have been starting a conversation with him.

Some people think they can train or threaten their partner into becoming who they want him or her to be. But honoring is based on respecting who a person is, not trying to train or coerce them into becoming the person you *want* them to be. If you are insisting, hoping, praying, or pressuring someone to be anyone other than who they are right now, you are not honoring them. You are also not honoring yourself.

To Treat Someone with Regard Is to Recognize Their Choice

Recently we were talking with a lady who was convinced that her partner would be more successful in his work if he upgraded his image and the way he dressed, so she started buying him a continuous stream of new shirts and giving him advice about which shoes and pants he should choose. But her efforts to enhance his image were not welcome. They represented *her* taste, not *his*. He liked the easy-going clothes he chose for himself. She was not honoring him; she was trying to "improve" him.

She asked us, "I know it's honoring of people to only give them what they can receive. But what can you do when you care about someone and you know you can contribute to them in a particular way, and they can't receive it? I find it challenging not to give someone everything I know is possible."

You may see the choices someone could have. You may see how they need to do something different, or how they could be different, and what that might look like, but that doesn't mean it's possible for them, in the moment, to perceive that they could be, do, or have that—or if they would ever desire to choose that. You perceiving a possibility for someone does not mean it is the "correct" choice.

You have to let people choose for themselves. You may think that offering someone everything you know is possible for them will give them a willingness to choose something great, but that's not how it works. Most people aren't willing to have unlimited possibilities as an awareness. They may look at their choices and say, "I don't have any choices." It's like someone who is being abused saying, "I have no choice. I have to eat shit." No, you don't have to eat shit. You can choose something else!

But you are not treating others with regard when you try to give them more than they're willing to receive. When you attempt to do that, they have to return it to you with daggers attached. Have you ever given someone a gift and had them ask, "What do you mean by this?" Or have you ever offered a friend an idea that could help with a problem and they said, "You have no idea what I need"? You might have felt surprised or offended by their response, you were only trying to help, but the fact is you were not honoring them when you attempted to give them more than they could accept.

You have to recognize what people can choose and what they can't choose. You have to allow everything to be what it is at the time and allow it to change when it changes, and if it changes—not because *you* want it to change, but because *they* choose to make a change. Often, we try to get our partner to choose something different because we have judged that that is the way they should be. There is no choice in this for either of you.

Total intimacy is a place in which you trust that you and the other person have choice at all times. You want to live from the place of total choice. That's the whole idea of intimacy.

Honoring yourself and others builds over time as you are aware of what's required in the moment. You become aware of what's required for them tomorrow and the day after that, and the day after that, and the day after that, and you build a platform of the intimacy that is actually possible.

Changing the World with Big Choices

You, as an infinite being, are the creator of everything in your life: the good, the bad, and the ugly. You create your reality by the choices you make. One of the biggest ways we dishonor ourselves is by judging our choices as small, and as a result, we believe our choices don't change anything—when, in fact, each choice can change everything.

Rather than choosing something that would change the world, we dishonor our infinite being in favor of small choices. We figure that with little choices, we won't create havoc in our life, so we buy other people's points of view and choose what they're choosing. We play small and do our best to fit in. But why would you make other people's points of view more real than your capacity to choose? That is the ultimate dishonoring of yourself as an infinite being.

What's a big choice? Many years ago, Dain was talking with Gary about getting a new car. He was considering what kind of car he would like to have and could afford, and asked Gary what he would suggest.

Gary replied, "When you buy a new car, the moment you drive it off the lot, it is instantaneously worth 10,000 dollars less than you paid for it. Why don't you buy a car that is a year or two old? That way, you'll be able to get a good deal on the car you truly want."

Dain said, "Good idea. I can afford this much, and I would like to have a sporty-looking convertible."

Gary asked him, "Why don't you try an Audi? They are great looking cars; they are sporty and they´ve got speed." So, Dain went to look at an Audi, but he didn't like them very much. He tried some other convertibles, but they weren´t what he wanted, either, then he tried a BMW convertible, which was a much bigger choice than he had ever considered. Dain got into the BMW and started driving, and immediately declared, "This is what I want!" He bought the car and laughed with delight and glee all the way home. He loved that car; it expanded his universe!

Not long after purchasing the BMW, Dain went to visit his family. He had previously told them about Access Consciousness, and they had never paid any attention and had no interest in learning more. However, when he showed up in his BMW, suddenly everyone wanted to know about Access Consciousness and what he was doing to be able to create such a thing. Buying the BMW was a choice that was big enough to get people interested in a different possibility.

Sometimes making choices that create significant changes in your life can be uncomfortable, but if you wish to change something in a big way, you must be willing to see what your choice will create in the world. With the willingness to make that choice, you instantaneously create a different possibility. You create something that changes your world and the people around you. When you do this, others can see that a different choice is available for them and invites them to know that they can make big choices as well.

Our Choice Creates

One of the biggest things about treating ourselves, others and the Earth with regard is realizing that our choice creates. Choice can even create big changes on a planetary scale. Unfortunately, instead of honoring the Earth and treating it with respect, many of us treat it disrespectfully. We don't look into how we can nurture it or care for it. We make small choices about taking care of it. Taking care of it is all about the judgment of what we think we are doing to the Earth, not seeing what is required for true nurturing and longevity. We use it. We abuse it. If you are willing to treat the Earth with regard and honor it, you will perceive and choose the world-changing choices that would be nurturing for it and allow it to nurture us back for generations.

People often talk about wanting to create intimate relationships with others, but usually they don't have a clue about how to honor themselves and still treat another person with regard. Being nice and treating someone with regard are not necessarily the same thing. And it's not about being nice. It's about being aware. To honor someone is to be aware of that person and to treat them the way *they* wish to be treated—not the way *you* think they should be treated.

This too is about making little choices rather than big ones, and in the process of doing that, you dishonor your infinite being. You create a little choice like "I love this person," and then you try to create an intimate relationship based solely on that without ever asking another question. It's all based on a conclusion. Where is the awareness? Where are the questions? You never ask, "Can I live with this person?" Instead, you say, "I love him. He's really annoying, but I'm sure we'll figure it out." You never ask, "Why do I stay with her?" You say, "But I love her."

These are little choices. Everything is based on: "I love him" or "I love her." You make 8,000 little choices around the small choice of, "I love him," none of which has the capacity to create a greater reality. Here are some questions that can assist with creating greater:

- Is this going to work?
- Am I coming to a conclusion? If yes, what is the conclusion I am coming to here?

If you are functioning from any form of conclusion when you start a relationship, you'll kill it. You have no choice; you have to kill it—because you've already made a decision and reached a conclusion. When you reach a conclusion about your relationship or your partner, you are limiting them, you and what is possible. Conclusion doesn't allow you to see things as they are. You are hoping for what you've defined as relationship instead of creating the relationship that is possible with this person. Ask instead:

- What's really possible here?
- What do I truly want with this person?
- Will this person be an addition to my life?

- Will I be an addition to their life?
- What's it going to be like if we do this together?

Most of us don't ask those kinds of questions. Be aware! Ask questions!

A relationship is something that should expand your life, not something that contracts it. What if you were always willing to be yourself and to state your desires? And what if you always honored yourself as well as your partner?

Putting the Tools of Honor into Practice

Many of us rarely factor ourselves into the equation of our own lives. We tend to think we have to lose ourselves or change who we truly are to create a relationship with another person. We constantly do things for other people and make them more important than ourselves. We give up ourselves in favor of their points of view and desires. We think that by knowing what they need, want, and desire, we are going to make them happy with us. This may be something you have tried to do. But did it work? Unfortunately, no, because no one can be happy with us if they are not happy with themselves. And we cannot be happy with another if we are not happy with ourselves.

What if there was a way to honor yourself and put yourself back into the equation of your life? What if there was a way to become more intimate with yourself, and as a result, the other people in your life? There is!

Start by Asking These Questions

- Do I listen to what I know, no matter what?
    - Write down some examples of how you have done that recently.
    - If you see that you haven't been listening to what you know, write down some examples of what you have done instead.
- Do I judge what I know?
    - What could you become aware of if you didn't judge the information?
- Do I acknowledge the gift and the brilliance of me?
    - Write down some examples of how you have done that.
    - And, if applicable, some examples of how you haven't.
- Am I willing to build a level of intimacy with myself where I become the priority in my life?
- What might that look like for you?

- What would treating myself with regard look like?
- What are some of the ways I honor myself?
- What are some of the ways I dishonor myself?
- What would my life be like if I treated myself with regard from the moment I got up in the morning to the time I went to bed?
- What would my life be like if I honored myself in every choice I made?

Questions You Can Ask Yourself Every Day

- How could I honor myself today?
- What choices can I make today to honor and nurture myself?
- What would create more ease for me?
- What would be fun for me today?
- How am I doing at honoring myself?

Now, ask yourself the same questions about your partner. Really look at this. Include examples of when you have, or haven't, done this.

- Do I listen to him or her, no matter what?
    - What is it like when I listen?
    - And what is it like when I don't?

- Am I judging him or her for their choices?
- Do I acknowledge the gift and the brilliance of him or her?
    - How do I do that?
    - How does he or she respond when I do that?
    - What does it look like when I don't do that?
- Am I willing to build a level of intimacy with him or her?
- What would treating him or her with regard look like?
- What are some of the ways I honor him or her?
- What are some of the ways I dishonor him or her?
- What would my life be like if I treated my partner with regard from the moment they got up in the morning to the time they went to bed?
- What would my life be like if I honored my partner in every choice they made?

If you wish, you can also ask yourself the same questions about others in your life: your kids, family members, friends, colleagues, and co-workers. Try it at least once and see what happens.

Additional Questions You Can Ask Yourself Every Day in Regard to Your Partner

- How could I honor this person today?
- What choices can I make today to honor and nurture this person?
- What would create more ease for this person in their situation?
- What would be fun for them today?

CHAPTER 2

Trust

Trust is usually understood to mean belief in the integrity, ability or character of a person, so when people talk about trust they say things like, "I trust employees to do a good job" or "I trust my kids to tell the truth." And when they talk about trust in relationships, they often say, "I trust my partner to be faithful to me."

Mary believed in the importance of trust in relationships, too, but she had a world-changing point of view about what trust looked like. One day when she and Gary were talking, she said, "I trust Bill to be who he is and to do what is right for himself. I trust him to be true to himself and to honor me in whatever way he can."

That didn't look anything like I had seen or considered previously! Most people think that trust means something like, "I trust my partner to keep their promises." It's some version of, "I trust this person to always do what I want and expect them to do."

Mary's point of view was "Trust is knowing that people are always going to do what they're going to do. It's looking at who the other person is, not who you wish, hope, pray, or pretend they're going to be."

Trust Is Not Blind Faith

Trust is not about having blind faith in someone, expecting them to be everything you want them to be, or assuming they'll do everything you want them to do. It's not thinking he is always going to put you first or that she will always do what she can to make you happy. It is simply knowing that the other person will do what he or she is going to do.

If he always leaves the toilet seat up, you trust he is going to do that. You don't have blind faith for him to put it down and then get pissed off when he doesn't. If she spends all the money on clothes, you trust she is going to do that. You don't freak out when she comes home with a new wardrobe. If he lies, you trust that he will lie—because the one thing you can trust about liars is they will lie. You trust your partner to be who he or she is, not who you want them to be.

People whose partners are alcoholics tend to have blind faith that the alcoholic will change because he or she loves them. They expect the alcoholic to become sober because of the relationship. But when you trust an alcoholic to stop drinking, you're destroying your own awareness. *You're making what you want greater than your awareness of what is.* Trust is being aware that your partner is an alcoholic and as such, he or she is going to drink until they choose differently. No amount of love or blind faith can override someone's choice.

We know a woman whose view of her partner was, "He's wonderful. He's fabulous. Now, if I could just get him to change!" She went ahead and married him, then got angry because he didn't change in the way she had "trusted" him to change. But that wasn't trust. Blind faith, hopes and wishes are not trust. Trust is, "This person is never going to be any different than they are right now, unless they choose to change something."

Trust that if you get into a relationship with someone who was cheating on his ex-wife, he'll probably cheat on you, too. Trust that if she cheated on her former husband and then she went with you, she's probably going to do that again, and decide from there whether that's the person you want in your life.

When you go to hopes, dreams, wishes, and blind faith instead of the kind of trust we are talking about here, you're choosing not to be aware. You're putting your faith in something that you don't actually believe is true. That's never your best choice. Have you ever heard someone say, "I like this person so I'm going to trust him?" What they're really saying is, "I am not going to be aware." When you do hopes, dreams, wishes, and blind faith you turn off your awareness to the person you are in a relationship with. And when you're not aware, how can you trust yourself?

Deal Breakers

Are we saying that you have to be alright with someone who cheats on you or abuses you? No. This can be a deal breaker.

A deal breaker is not a judgment; it's an awareness. Most people use deal breakers as a way to justify walking away after they've already invalidated what they knew from the beginning of the relationship. Or they use them as ultimatums, "You need to change this, or else." Neither of those come from trust or awareness. A true deal breaker is simply recognizing what you are willing and unwilling to live with, and honoring that without making the other person or yourself wrong.

If you know someone lies and you require honesty, that's not judgment, that's awareness. If you know someone drinks, cheats, abuses money, or refuses to take responsibility for their choices, and you know that doesn't work for you, the question is not how to get them to change. The question is, are you willing to be in a relationship with them as they are right now?

Deal breakers are not about making someone wrong for who they are. They're about being honest with yourself about what you can choose while still maintaining your integrity, your joy, and your awareness. The problem is when people pretend that they don't have deal breakers. They say things like, "I'm so open, I have no judgement," or "I am in total allowance," when in reality, they're just avoiding making a choice. Allowance doesn't mean you have to stay or go; allowance is recognizing what is. Then making a choice accordingly.

If someone continually violates your trust, dismisses your awareness, or requires you to diminish yourself to stay in the relationship, that is them telling you who they are, and that is information. Information to choose from, not a problem to fix.

You don't need to justify leaving or staying. You don't need to convince anyone that your deal breakers are valid. And importantly, you don't need to wait until things get unbearable to honor them. When you're willing to acknowledge your deal breakers early, relationships become lighter, easier, and kinder. You stop trying to fit it with what this reality says is a successful relationship. You stop hoping someone will become different.

That is trusting yourself. That is where real intimacy begins.

Testing Your Partner

Sometimes when people are not functioning from their awareness, they create situations that put others through different kinds of tests. In other words, they are in doubt, consciously or unconsciously, about the other person, and they make him or her jump through hoops to "prove" their trustworthiness. If you trust your partner to be who they are, you wouldn't have to test them. You are only testing them because you know somewhere you have made a hopeful judgment of them.

We know a guy who was so worried about his partner cheating on him that he asked a friend of his to "test" her by flirting with her and asking her out. (She refused his invitation.) Sometimes people create a test by taking someone they are dating to a family gathering, so they can get family members to check that person out. That's another kind of test. Or they continuously ask the person questions about their past, while being on the lookout for inconsistencies in their answers.

If the person they're testing passes whatever the final test is, they say, "Okay, she has proved she is trustworthy," or "I know I can trust that he is going to do *x, y, z.*" This can create some significant relationship difficulties for people because they are thinking, "I don't have to be aware anymore." They come out of awareness and go into blind faith that the other person will be everything they decided he or she would or should be.

If you have to get somebody to prove to you that they are trustworthy, you are creating a competition designed to make the other person lose. Unfortunately, this is the way many people do relationships. Or they attempt to prove they're more aware than the other person. Or that they're the one who has the right point of view. Have you ever set your partner up to lose? In truth, you haven't, because functioning from a win-lose scenario ensures that both of you lose.

In the end, the one who loses the competition gives in to the other person's point of view. He or she says, "Okay, I'm not going to fight this anymore." This is what happens with many relationships, and it destroys true intimacy. True intimacy is knowing that you can trust the other person to be who he or she is. Consider the ease, respect and regard that comes from Mary and Bill's way of creating trust with awareness, versus attempts to test, control, outsmart, or manipulate the other person.

Living with Integrity

With intimacy, trust doesn't just involve trusting others. It is also about trusting yourself. When you're willing to trust in yourself, you know whether other people are trustworthy because you are functioning from awareness and integrity with yourself. You honor your awareness and your knowing of what works for you.

Integrity is being true to your own reality. It's walking your talk. It's doing what you say you are going to do. You don't break your agreements, and you don't do things for the sake of the other person. You do these things for yourself—because you have integrity. When somebody says to you, "You know that agreement you made? It's not legally binding. You don't really have to do that," you say, "Well, that may be, but I can't live with myself if I break my agreements." Integrity with yourself is the number one thing you need to have.

Wouldn't you rather keep on top of what you agree to do rather than not doing it? Carry through, always. If you agree to do something, do it. It doesn't matter whether it's going to work out well for you, because it's not about what you want. It is about the way you always conduct yourself, and as a result, you can always feel good about yourself.

Sometimes people ask, "How do you cope when you're functioning with integrity and no one else around you is doing that?" We say, "It doesn't matter how other people are functioning because what you do, you do for *you*. When the people around you do their lack-of-integrity thing, you say, "Okay, you chose that. That's not what I'm going to choose."

You do what you say you're going to do. You have the willingness to walk your talk, which is why people trust you. If you have said you'll do something, even if it appears to be detrimental to you, you still do it. Why would you do that? Because that's what works for you? Or because that's what works for other people? You do it because that's what works for you! You're trying to do the best you can at all times. And if you do make the mistake of not choosing integrity in a given situation, you own it. You admit it to yourself, apologize to others if that's appropriate, make up any damage you might have done, and resolve to choose integrity in the future.

Inherited Distrust of Self

Trusting yourself, being true to your own values and your way of seeing the world, is an essential part of having integrity. Integrity is being true to your own reality. What is your reality?

Did you have parents who didn't function from being themselves? They didn't say, "Whatever I am, I'll be true to that. I will let my kids be true to whatever they are and whatever they choose." Instead, they functioned from the image they were trying to create—the image of being a good parent, perhaps, or whatever it was for them—and they tried to mold you in their image. It isn't malicious, and sometimes it isn't done cognitively. It's how they were taught to parent.

You may have grown up with people who didn't see who you were or who didn't have the ability to acknowledge you and your capacities. They didn't recognize and appreciate what was different about you. They thought that, in order to prove the rightness of their unawareness, they had to dominate and control you. Many of the people around us did this. They weren't truly themselves; they didn't trust themselves; they didn't learn to trust themselves—and you came to believe that you, too, could have no trust in being yourself.

When you grow up with somebody who has the point of view that you're not trustworthy, somebody who doesn't have the level of awareness you have, who doesn't have the level of caring you have, who doesn't have the level of kindness you have, who doesn't have the level of brilliance you have, you end up invalidating yourself. You stop trusting yourself. You think, "If they can't trust me, surely I must be untrustworthy."

Because you´re a kid, you aren't able to look at that person and say, "Wow! This person is choosing to be so much less of a being than I'm willing to be." You think you can't have that point of view about somebody who has a bigger body and is supposed to care about you and know more than you. You invalidate yourself rather than functioning from your awareness and seeing what is actually true for you.

When we allow someone who is unconscious or anti-conscious to dominate our life by enforcing their views of right and wrong on us, we don't learn to trust what's actually true for us. We don't trust our own knowing. Many of us have had in our lives people who, for whatever reason, did whatever they could to destroy the kindness and the greatness of us, as it was most likely destroyed in them. They tried to kill our trust in ourselves. That's one of the effects of abuse. But what if you had the capacity to undo all of that and to restore your trust in yourself?

One of the easiest ways to restore trust in yourself is to go back through your life and recall those times where you knew you weren't wrong—times when something occurred that told you that you were wrong, and you believed it. Even then, it might be hard to say, "Wow, I was right!" because you've been told your whole life that you're wrong, one way or another. What if you were never wrong and what if you were never right?

Become a Beacon of Trust

People tell us that one of the things they love about Access Consciousness is being around people who they trust and who trust them. People who have their back. Some of them say, "This is the first time in my life I've had this."

Part of functioning from your awareness is being a beacon of trust and integrity. People see your integrity and they trust you. It allows them to know that trust exists in the world. Embodying trust and all the elements of intimacy, you demonstrate it and invite others to know that it is possible for them. What if part of what you're here to contribute to the world is an awareness of what true intimacy is?

When you're willing to function from more awareness of yourself, more intimacy becomes available with others. You're no longer doing it from judgment, projections, expectations and filters, you're trusting them to be exactly who they are. You're allowing them to see you, and they allow you to see them.

Putting the Tools of Trust into Practice

What if you trusted yourself? What if you trusted your past choices? What if everything you thought was a wrongness about you was a strongness? The truth is that you have chosen every single thing you have done to get to where you are today. What if you did this so you would be able to create something different? You couldn't have chosen wrong. You're an infinite being and infinite beings don't choose wrong. They just choose strong.

At one point, Gary was looking at all the different kinds of jobs he had done in his life – everything from dealing in antiques and real estate to breeding horses. He thought, "Wow, I've done one useless job after another. I don't have a commitment to anything." Then he realized that every one of those so-called useless jobs had set him up for everything he does today. He saw that he had been making his past experience wrong when there was actually something very right about it.

This is something you may have done as well. Instead of looking at your past and saying, "This was a terrible experience!" here are two questions you can ask:

- **What's right about that situation or experience that I'm not getting?**

- **What did I gain from that experience that I haven't acknowledged?**

It doesn't matter whether the experience was difficult and awful or fun or brilliant or wonderful. That's not the point. The question is:

- **What did I gain from that experience that I haven't acknowledged?**

Look at your life and see what you have done and what you have accomplished, what you went after and what you let go of. Look at it all and ask:

- **If I combined all this stuff, what could I create in the world that hasn't yet been created?**

Have you suffered abuse or been through terrible things? Don't go to, "Oh, I have had a terrible life!" Stop trying to make your life wrong. Are you dead? Are you in the grave? No. Then obviously, you got strong from your experience. You chose that experience to get that strength. Now how are you going to use it? What are you going to create with it? Ask:

- **What strongness am I not acknowledging?**
- **What did I gain from that experience that I can use to help others?**

- **What did I learn, or what did I know, or where did I get to, that I've never acknowledged?**

You have gotten to places you've never acknowledged. What would it be like if you were willing to have all that and trust in it?

Tool: What's right about me that I'm not getting?

When Gary was young, he had two best friends. He introduced them to each other, thinking they could all play together. Instead, the two boys became close friends and left Gary out. He came away from that experience saying, "I will never treat anyone like that, ever! No one should have to experience that kind of pain and suffering." Instead of making himself wrong and limiting his choice in friendship based on their choices, his choice was to create something different with people in the future.

It doesn't matter what you chose. You have to stop making yourself wrong. You're working hard to see something wrong with everything you've chosen. Instead, start using the question: *What's right about me that I'm not getting?* Use it nonstop for the next month. Every time you start to look for something that is wrong about you, ask that question because there is something right about you that you're not getting.

It can be so easy to get swept into the wrongness of you, especially in a world so full of judgment. Here are few more questions you can ask whenever you catch yourself judging your choices as wrong:

- **What strongness am I not acknowledging?**
- **What did I gain from that experience that I can use to help others?**
- **What did I learn, or what did I know, or where did I get to, that I've never acknowledged?**
- **What else is possible here?**

Tool: Choose Something Different

Have you noticed that we often get into the habit of choosing the same thing over and over again? It's as if we think that if we do it often enough, we're going to get a different result. We choose the same type of people to have relationships with, the same kind of work situations, the same kind of problems and difficulties, the same kind of lapses in integrity—and we end up with the same kind of regrets. The beginning of trusting yourself is knowing that you can choose something different. You can say, "I don't have to choose this again. I can choose something else," and then you do. Recognize that every time you choose something different, everybody around you has to choose something different as well.

Your choice to do something different is not about defending for or against anything. It's simply choosing to do something different, making another choice. It doesn't matter what anyone else's point of view about you is. Why would you make their point of view more important than what you know is true for you?

When we choose to defend ourselves against the dominance of other people's points of view, we think we can protect or guard ourselves, or we can do something that will get the abusive person to change or stop what they're doing. Or we think we can give in and then they will stop trying to dominate us. None of that works. What you have to do is choose something different. This creates a place where the other person has to change. They have no choice but to change because you are no longer being the person who buys their judgment about you as real and true.

You made a choice and that choice created a result. Know that you can always choose again, and by your choice, you will at least change the situation. Recognize you can always choose something that will change things.

Trust that you have choice. Ask, "What choice can I make that would change this?" Then make the choice and see how it works. You will discover: "Oh! I can choose. I can choose something that will change this situation." You are not looking for what's good, or right, or perfect, or correct. That is all judgment. You're not trying to control anything or anyone. It's simply:

- **What choice can I make that will change this?**
- **What choice is available that would change this situation?**

CHAPTER 3

Allowance

The third element of great intimacy is allowance. This is about allowing yourself and others to be as they are. Allowance doesn't require your approval, agreement or admiration of others. You are simply willing for them to be whatever or however they are.

When you are in allowance, you don't buy the idea that what another person is saying or doing has to affect you. You don't resist and react, nor do you criticize and argue or try to stop the other person from being different than you. Nor do you align and agree with the other person and try to make them your whole life. You have a life. And you let the other person have a life.

Allowance is knowing that everything is just an interesting point of view, which is seeing something not with judgement but just as it is. When you're in allowance, thoughts, ideas, beliefs, attitudes, judgments, and emotions come at you, and you're like a rock in the stream. Everything flows around you, and you're still you. But if you start to resist and react or align and agree with those thoughts, ideas, beliefs, attitudes, judgments, or emotions, you get swept away in the current and you are lost.

Resistance and reaction is being angry, critical or judgmental about things, while alignment and agreement is going along with it passively. The other choice is to be in allowance, which is: "That's an interesting point of view." This is where you realize that whatever you or the other person is doing, it's just a choice. They have a choice and you have a choice. You can be upset about that choice, or you can think it's a wonderful choice, or you can be in allowance of whatever the choice is.

It's about allowing the other person to have their own beliefs and points of view, to do things the way they do them, and to believe and behave as they choose. You recognize and acknowledge that you have your life and your reality, while the other person has their life and their reality.

Mary and Bill had great allowance for one another, and it was important to them that the other person had his or her own point of view. Mary said, "When Bill and I would go on too long discussing things we didn't agree on, Bill would say, 'Okay, Mary, the complaint department is now closed.'" This meant, "We're not going to talk about this any longer." Mary knew it was time for her to allow Bill to have his point of view, and for him to allow her to have hers. They weren't going to agree on the issue. They would simply agree to disagree.

When Gary heard that, he said, "Wow! My wife gets outraged when I don't agree with her. She goes off on people all the time because she believes everyone needs to see and agree with her point of view, regardless of what theirs is."

Allowance Keeps the Space of You Available to You

Toward the end of Bill's life, he developed Alzheimer's and began to lose his memory. He would ask Mary a question and five minutes later, he'd ask the same question again. He would answer the phone, talk to the caller, offer to take a message then completely forget the person had called. He couldn't keep track of what day of the week it was or where Mary had gone when she went to the store, even though she had told him several times before leaving where she was going.

He also forgot things about himself. Bill had been a chain smoker from the time he was a young man. Once after he began to lose his memory, he went into the hospital for a few days and wasn't allowed to smoke while he was there. By the time he returned home, he had completely forgotten about smoking. Mary was delighted with that turn of events. She threw away his cigarettes and thought that was the end of the matter; however, a couple of days later Bill was watching TV and saw someone smoking. Suddenly he remembered smoking and had to have a cigarette.

None of these things fazed Mary. She was completely in allowance of what was happening with Bill. She was incredibly caring and kind with him and simply allowed him to be the way he was. She didn't judge him. She didn't resist and react to his lapses of memory, nor did she get swept away in a current of emotions, thoughts, ideas, beliefs, attitudes, and judgments about his condition.

Gary knew several other women whose husbands had Alzheimer's, and they had become mean and nasty toward their spouses. They would shout things like, "I already told you that three times! Can't you remember anything?" These women were in resistance and reaction. Others went into alignment and agreement with their husbands' illness and treated them like babies or unfortunate victims. They tearfully said things like, "Oh, honey, I'm so sorry this has happened to you. This is terrible. Here, let me help you."

Not Mary! She was totally present and aware with Bill until the end of his life, and her kindness was beyond anything Gary had ever seen. She would repeat the same thing ten times for Bill if that's what it took. She said, "Bill can't remember things anymore, so I can't expect him to remember things. That would be cruel." She didn't have a point of view about it. It simply was what it was. She was in total allowance.

What if you could have that kind of allowance in your relationship? What if you didn't resist and react to the other person's point of view, or align and agree with it, but simply allowed the point of view to be what it was: just an interesting point of view? Allowance is the kindness of being with what is happening, regardless of your ideas about it. For Mary, it was simply: "Bill can't remember things anymore. Okay. I can't expect him to do that."

Allowance Is NOT Being a Doormat

Sometimes people think being in allowance means you have to be a doormat or let others walk all over you. Nothing could be further from the truth. Allowance isn't the same as acceptance or approval. When you're in allowance, you create a space for other people to have their points of view and for you to have yours. You recognize that you don't have to change yourself in response to other people's points of view. And you don't expect others to change themselves in response to yours.

There was a period of time, years ago, when Gary's son would visit when he was drunk, and when he was drunk, he became obnoxious and unpleasant. One day Gary said to him, "I don't like you when you drink. You're not that much fun to be with and I would rather not be around you when you do it. Could you not come here when you've been drinking?"

His son asked, "Where's your allowance, Dad?"

Gary said, "This is allowance. I haven't told you to stop drinking. I haven't gotten angry or criticized you or treated you badly. I've simply asked that you not come over when you're drunk because I am not interested in being abused." Gary wasn't functioning from alignment and agreement or resistance and reaction. He wasn't trying to control his son. He was coming from the awareness that his son's behavior didn't work for him. In asking his son to not be around him while drunk, Gary chose what worked for him, while his son chose what worked for him.

Eventually Gary's son did stop drinking and started visiting again, and they developed a much better relationship than they had before because there was space in the relationship for each of them to be who they were, which is the whole point of allowance.

There Is No Judgment in Allowance

Sometimes people think that if you're functioning from total allowance and "interesting point of view," you're not being caring. That is a misunderstanding of what caring actually is. When you truly care for yourself, you realize that whatever the other person does, it has to be their choice, and you create a totally different reality. You take care of yourself and at the same time allow the other person to be exactly who they are and to do exactly what they do. This is a true expression of caring. Allowance is actually the most caring place from which to function because there is no judgment in it. You are in awareness rather than reaction.

A lot of people have a mistaken idea of what caring actually is, and they use "caring" as a way to control their partner, their friends or their kids. They say things like, "Oh, honey, I'm sorry, but I can't let you go camping with your friends. What if you got hurt? I love you so much and I could never forgive myself if that happened." This is control disguised as caring.

Others try to use anger to intimidate or control the people around them. If their partner or their child does something they don't like, they blow up or have a temper tantrum. They get critical or refuse to listen. They may even threaten violence. In allowance, you are not trying to control anybody.

Allowance is: "Everything is just an interesting point of view."

When Dain was a little kid, one of his grandfather's warehouse managers quit smoking and decided that everyone in the world needed to quit as well. He had no allowance whatsoever for anyone who smoked. If he caught anyone smoking in the warehouse, he would walk up to the person, get in his face, and blast him with, "Don't you know what you're doing? You could *DIE*!" This is anger and judgment, not caring.

Until we truly get what allowance is, we all do some version of what the warehouse manager did. We get annoyed or pissed off at people for the things they do. We get in their face. We try to dominate and control them. You'll find life gets a lot easier when you live a life from allowance.

When you're in allowance of yourself, you're willing to change anything. If you have a problem, you're in allowance of yourself that you've created it and from there you can change it. But if you're not in allowance you keep trying to see how the problem can be blamed on somebody else, and in so doing, you eliminate your capacity to generate and create something different.

"Everything Should Go My Way" Is Not Allowance

Have you ever had to call a company for customer service where you've had to call them five or six times only to get agents that don't have the ability to help you? At the end of that experience, were you upset, angry and annoyed that things didn't go your way? That's not exactly allowance.

"Everything should go my way" is not allowance and it is not awareness. It's a fixed point of view that's not going to get you anywhere. You have to realize, "Oh, I've got a fixed point of view about the way this should turn out." Once you do that, you can start asking questions and you'll see that other options are available. Until then, you're stuck in resistance and reaction.

Allowance is a creative energy. It is not passive. It is never a stop. It is never a judgment. It is always a question. Allowance opens up possibilities, because that's what a question does. Once you get to allowance, all the possibilities are there for the choosing. Conversely, alignment and agreement, resistance and reaction destroy all possibilities. It always leads to *stop*, never to *start,* and never to *more.*

Employers often face challenges to their allowance when employees don't create exactly what they ask for. The employer then addresses it with frustration and withdrawal. How much allowance is in them doing that? None. They are not in allowance of themselves or their employee because they were trying to make the employee do something they weren't inclined to do. You can't make people do what you want, you have to see what they are willing to do and go there.

"What I'm Doing Isn't Working"

When someone says they're going to do something, does that mean they're going to do it? No. It just means they said they would do it. You have to be in allowance of the fact that most people lie, even to themselves.

When you've requested somebody to do something and it appears they haven't done it, do you ask? When they say they didn't do it, what if you moved on, without judgment? You don't question why they chose not to do it, why they wouldn't do it, or any other question designed to make them justify their choice. You could choose to be in allowance of them and practice honoring yourself in knowing that what you're doing isn't working.

Let People Make Their Own Mistakes

If you don't have allowance, you have no choice but to resist and react. And if you're in resistance and reaction to your partner, your family, your kids, or the people you work with, you have no opportunity to choose something different.

You may think you have to prove that someone is wrong or that they're right, one way or the other, but neither one of those has anything to do with choice. You may say, "Well, I know best." That would be a conclusion, which has nothing to do with awareness. You may say, "I have little allowance for people choosing the crap they choose, and I know it won't work well for them in the future, so I try to convince them..." That's a big mistake. You can never convince anybody about anything.

Allowance is: You let people make their own mistakes. Allowance is: You let them figure it out for themselves. Allowance is: You know that they may never get it right. Don't kill yourself trying to help someone get it right, because all they're going to do is make you wrong.

Withdrawing Is Just a Another Way of Trying to Prove That You're Right

Gary can always see when somebody's making a mistake. He will not say anything unless they ask him a question, but at the same time, he doesn't withdraw from them. Withdrawing is just a way of proving you're right. Rightness is just rightness. Rightness is cool. Gary loves being right. He loves being able to tell people, "I told you so," but that doesn't usually create what he would like to create, so he doesn't do it.

Have you noticed that people don't listen? Does that annoy and frustrate you? You would like them to listen to you so they see how smart you are, except nobody wants to know how smart *you* are. They only want to know how smart *they* are. Realize that other people's lives are about *them*. Everything becomes a lot easier if you recognize that.

Total Allowance and Awareness

When you are operating from total allowance and awareness, greater possibilities can occur in all areas of your life. You have no judgment of anything. You're not willing to cut off your awareness in favor of your point of view, and as a result, you have total clarity in every aspect of your life.

What would it take for you to operate from total allowance and awareness, and to create great intimacy with your partner and with everything and everyone in your life?

Putting the Tools of Allowance into Practice

Tool: Where Have I Been There and Done That?

You may not yet realize it, but you have the capacity to be the energy of allowance twenty-four hours a day, seven days a week. What's required to have that? Whenever you become aware that you're judging someone or something, recognize that the only reason you're judging them is because you've got that in *you* someplace. Then ask, "Where have I been there and done that?"

You might be surprised by what comes up when you ask this question and the changes it can produce. Try it when your kids are driving you crazy or when you feel like yelling at a neighbor or a colleague.

Question: What Really Annoys Me?

People love to tell Gary and Dain about the one thing that really annoys them, the thing they have absolutely no allowance for. It might be when "spiritual" people project their airy-fairy points of view on them, or when somebody tells them what they need to do. What annoys *you*? Realize that whatever it is, you wouldn't be in such resistance to it if you hadn't done something like that yourself at some point.

Tool: Everything I Was That Made Me Like That in Any Lifetime, I Destroy and Uncreate It.

Let's say you work with a colleague who makes a lot of mistakes, and you have to regularly check her work. You've talked with her about the mistakes and she changes for a little while and then begins to make the same sort of mistakes all over again. You start judging her. You conclude that she's stupid. You begin to get angry, furious, and hateful. There might even be part of you that loves having this anger against her.

There's a good chance that somebody who screws up that much is angry and suppressing the anger. So, what do you do with that? When you are with somebody who's angry, you can be in allowance of their anger. You could calmly ask your colleague, "Are you angry about something?"

If she asks, "What do you mean?" you could say, "Well, I've noticed that you tend not to do what you need to do with your work, and I wondered if there's something you're angry about."

If she starts getting defensive and asks, "Why would I be angry?!" you'll know she is indeed angry, and you can say, "I'm sorry. I apologize." Now you know that her anger is creating the screw-ups in her work because all her attention is on the thing she's angry about. At that point, you can go into allowance. Don't try to blame the mistakes on her being stupid. Judging and coming to conclusions doesn't help. What may well help is saying, "Everything I was that made *me* like that in any lifetime, I destroy and uncreate it."

Four Questions You Can Ask to Change Anything

- **What is this?**
- **What do I do with it?**
- **Can I change it?**
- **If so, how do I change it?**

Keep asking these four questions in sequence and the energy will begin to shift as you invite change. Let the awareness come to you however it comes. And remember, it may not look the way you expect it to!

Tool: Interesting Point of View

If you want to get *really* free, practice saying, "Interesting point of view I have this point of view" for every point of view you have about everything and everyone in your life—including yourself and your relationship. Do this for six weeks or six months and see what happens.

When you use this tool, you begin to see that everything is just a point of view you have taken for the time being. It doesn't mean anything. And you can change that point of view at any moment. If you can learn to live as "Interesting point of view," you can remain in allowance and stop getting caught up in the trauma, drama, upset, and intrigue that is going on around you.

You'll find life gets easier, more enjoyable and intimacy becomes possible when you start using these questions and tools and go into allowance.

Chapter 4

Vulnerability

Most of us have been taught that if we are vulnerable, we will be susceptible to physical or emotional harm, damage or injury. We see vulnerability as being weak, unprotected or defenseless, and believe that people will take advantage of us or hurt us in some way, so we try to make ourselves "right," because nobody wants to be wrong.

We'd like to offer another point of view: What if being vulnerable gives you access to the gifts, talents and abilities which you truly are, thereby allowing you to succeed in whatever it is you choose to do?

Here's another way to think about it: You are being vulnerable when you exist with no barriers or walls. Contrary to being the risky place you've been told it is, it's a place of total potency, power and capacity. When you are vulnerable, you see the greatness of others, and you are willing to let them be that… And at the same time, you are the greatness of you.

This reality tells us that in order to be *somebody* in this world, in order to be successful and important, in order to win and not lose, we have to create an image that gets people to see us in a certain desirable way. So we adopt an image. But here's the problem: When you create anything based on an image, whatever it happens to be, you have to put a lot of energy into maintaining and upholding it.

The opposite of this is vulnerability, which is saying, "Enough of the image! I am going to be me!"

Are you willing to let go of the image you have created, whatever it is, and truly have you, just the way you are? What would it be like to present yourself, as you are, to the world, to your partner, your family, your kids, your co-workers, and everybody else in your world?

When you are being vulnerable, you don't use barriers or walls to protect yourself, nor do you try to project the image of someone you think you're supposed to be. This kind of vulnerability is something that many of us have avoided. We've bought into the point of view: "I have to be tough. If I'm vulnerable, I won't be safe. I'll get hurt, or people will take advantage of me." But what if none of that is true? What if being vulnerable gives you access to the gifts, talents, and abilities that you truly are, thereby allowing you to succeed in your life and your relationships? What if vulnerability is a space of total potency, capacity, and power? And what if it's an essential element in creating great intimacy?

The first time Gary heard Mary say, "You have to be totally vulnerable with the other person," he, thought, "What?!" He was married at the time to a woman who had grown up seeing anger as a source of power, and whenever she got upset with him about something, she would direct huge amounts of anger at him. When she did that, all of his protective shields would go up. She would beat on him with her anger and Gary would stand there with his shields and defenses up until he either dropped the barriers or ran away. Mary encouraged him to become vulnerable no matter what, and he started forcing the barriers down when his wife directed anger at him.

People who are angry want someone to slam. They want something to beat on. If you go into allowance and vulnerability you take away the barrier or shield you have put in place to protect yourself, and you create a completely different reality. Without barriers, there's nothing for the other person's force to bump against, so it flows back to the person who is delivering it. You let the other person deliver whatever it is they are directing at you, and in a very short period of time the anger will dissipate. When Gary started doing this with his ex-wife, she would run out of steam in about three minutes, but if he kept his barriers in place, she could go on for hours.

If your partner, or anyone, comes at you with anger, simply push your barriers down and let their anger go through you. You are not absorbing it; you are letting it pass through without it affecting you. If you don't put up a barrier or a shield, people have nothing to bang against, and they don't have to exert force in trying to make themselves right. In fact, if somebody goes on and on at you, it's *because* you're keeping your barriers up. Lower the barriers or shove them out of the way, and he or she will run out of steam.

Force the Barriers Down

If you wish to create an extraordinary relationship, you have to notice when your automatic barriers go up and learn to keep them down. Recognize that anything the other person says or does is neither right or wrong, nor good or bad. It is just an interesting point of view.

When you are being truly vulnerable, you don't need to use barriers or walls to protect yourself. This kind of vulnerability is something that many of us have avoided. We've bought into the point of view "I have to be tough. If I'm vulnerable, people will take advantage of me."

But what if none of that is true? What if being vulnerable gives you access to the gifts, talents, and abilities you truly are, thereby allowing you to succeed in your life and your relationships? What if vulnerability is a space of total potency, capacity, and power? And what if it's an essential element in creating great intimacy? It is!

The Fear of Being Vulnerable

Most of us tend to resist and react to the idea of being vulnerable. The thought of exposing ourselves as we truly are is just too scary. We fear that we live in a crazy, dangerous world, and if we are vulnerable, we will be seen as weak and undesirable, or get hurt or criticized.

We often hear people say things like, "I'm afraid to be myself. I don't even know what I'm trying to protect. I'd like to meet someone I can be in communion with, but I'm scared to let anyone in. What if they don't like what they see?"

The truth is it doesn't matter whether or not somebody likes you, because if you're not willing to be vulnerable, to be as you are, you'll put up more than enough barriers to drive them away. And when you put up barriers, the only thing you create between you and the other person is distance.

No one can make you choose vulnerability. It's your choice. You have to choose it because you recognize that it's valuable. What would happen if you realized that everything in life, including your relationships, would work better for you if you did not have barriers up? Would you be willing to keep them down?

Barriers Don't Actually Protect Us

People tend to think that barriers protect them, but the opposite is true. Barriers are one of the ways we shut off our awareness and create a lockdown in our body. They're like the walls of a castle—barriers keep the invaders out. But they also keep us in, and they make us unable to receive the possibilities of a relationship.

Vulnerability is about lowering the barriers and perceiving who or what is in front of us. When we are vulnerable, we are willing to receive everything without judgment and without a fixed point of view. To be totally vulnerable is to not put up barriers to anyone or anything.

What if vulnerability is actually a strength? What if it gives you access to the gifts, talents and abilities that are truly *you?* What if vulnerability allows you to have truly intimate relationships with everyone and everything, including yourself?

There are many different kinds of barriers, and all of them are defense systems people use to protect themselves. Some people erect barriers to protect others from being hurt by their anger or sarcasm. That might sound well-intentioned, but it's not being vulnerable. It is judgment of yourself. Some people use their intellect as a barrier. They say, "You don't know as much as I do." Some people use their emotions as a barrier. They create emotional tirades with trauma and drama. They cry and say, "You don't understand me!" Other people use sex as a barrier. They will withhold sex saying, "Keep out! I'm not willing to receive any part of you."

Recognize that when you put up a barrier, you are blocking the other person from being present with you. You're in your own little world and you won't let them in. Putting up barriers is an attempt to control everything, because there is no solution to be found for the barrier you're putting up. Its sole purpose is to create separation between you and the other person so you don't have to communicate, and you don't have to have intimacy.

What can you do with barriers? You can recognize them when they start coming up and you say, "Oh! I'm putting my barriers up. I am going to choose to shove them down." You're willing to fight for yourself and your relationship by forcing the barriers out of existence. Be conscious enough to know it's a barrier and choose to get it down.

The truth is, if you are totally vulnerable, no one will ever hurt you.

Receiving Is Not Having Someone Dishonor You

We've said that vulnerability requires you to be present with yourself and to not put up barriers to receiving, but please note that when we say this, we are not talking about receiving a punch. Receiving is not having someone dishonor you.

In domestic violence situations, there is always a party that wants to make things better. However, you have to consider if the other person is willing to do that as well. If they are cheating on you and beating you up, this is not a relationship. It's abuse. Using the tool of allowance, you should look at whether you want to stay in this situation. Does this work for you? Truth, do I truly want to stay here?

Being vulnerable does not, by itself, change an abusive situation. You must have honor, trust, allowance, vulnerability, and gratitude for yourself before you can have a relationship with someone else. Look at what's occurring when there is abuse and see if you truly want to stay in that situation. If not, look at what the other choices and possibilities are.

Part of vulnerability is you have to be brutally honest with yourself. Look closely at what you want to choose, why you want to choose it, and what the value of choosing it is to you personally. You do this so you can determine where you want to go from there. It's part of creating the platform for how you exist in the world and how you create something greater for yourself and others. Being honest in this way is not about judging yourself. It's the way you get clear about yourself, your situation, and what you truly desire to have. You can do this.

When you are vulnerable, you are totally present in your life. You're totally willing to receive. You are willing to be honest about what is true for you. And you realize that wherever you put up a barrier, you disconnect from a part of you. You're no longer totally present with yourself.

Most people have the point of view that in order not to be hurt, you have to be invincible and invulnerable, but really, the only reason you get hurt is because you're not willing to be aware of what somebody would do that would hurt you. When you're truly aware you receive information about what's going to happen, how it's going to happen, and what it's going to look like.

Most people have been taught the idea of needing to fix what's broken, but when you function from vulnerability, things don't have the same chance of getting broken in the first place. You don't have barriers in place, so you have the awareness of things before they break. You know when you need to make changes long before you would when you're not vulnerable. The awareness comes like a feather touch across your cheek rather than a brick across the face because you don't have energetic debris in the way.

The value of being vulnerable is the ability to create anything and everything, because when you don't create from a fixed point of view, you can create something that's greater than anything that has existed before.

Vulnerability and Receiving

In this reality, you're taught that you're supposed to put up barriers so you can protect and define yourself. You think you're supposed to do this so you can live within the walls of the prescribed reality you have designed. So, you do that. And what happens? You end up feeling contracted, or like there's no space for you.

But are walls or barriers actually protection? Or are they a guarantee that somebody will fight with you? When you put up barriers, you have to contract and withdraw your awareness within the limits you've created. This makes you an easy target. And it is an amazingly difficult place from which to function.

When you allow yourself to open to the level of vulnerability we're talking about, your ability to receive increases in all areas of life. You have an awareness of what's really possible. You have the ability to create everything or anything at will. It's a much more fun place to be. Life is much easier. Your awareness is expanded and so is your receiving, which means you allow people to contribute to you. You open to receive what they offer you. And this kind of receiving creates a possibility for things to happen with total ease. Without walls and barriers, you can expand out and occupy a huge space. This is a key ingredient in creating intimacy.

Are You Willing to Have the Fantastic, the Phenomenal, and the Magnificent?

Have you chosen to be vulnerable? You choose not to be vulnerable all the time because in some way you believe that being present requires you to put up barriers. How many ways have you created a comfortable distance between *being* and *receiving*? You won't let yourself have anything greater than what you see in the world because you think that would be receiving too much. You consistently choose a low level of vulnerability and receiving that takes you back to the walls and limitations of your barriers, and never beyond them.

If you're willing to have the fantastic, the phenomenal and the magnificence that comes with the level of vulnerability that can occur, you're willing to receive everything. This is a level of vulnerability you can work towards. You aren't going to get there instantaneously, but you will get there when you allow yourself to choose more vulnerability each day.

Putting the Tools of Vulnerability into Practice

Tool: All of Life Comes to Me with Ease, Joy and Glory®

This is an Access Consciousness tool that will help you receive everything that comes to you, whether it has to do with your relationship or anything else in your world. What if everything—the good, the bad, the ugly—came to you with ease and joy and glory? And what if you received it all, without barriers or resistance? Would that create a different possibility in your life and in your relationships?

We call this tool the mantra of Access Consciousness because when you say it over and over again, things begin to happen differently. "All of life comes to me with ease, joy and glory."

Ease: Everybody gets that. Life doesn't have to be hard. When you have ease, you have joy.

Joy: It's fun. Joy is a higher energetic state or vibration that leads to glory.

Glory: An exuberant expression of abundance.

This little gem gives you the possibility to receive everything—all of life—including great intimacy. We recommend you say, "All of life comes to me with ease, joy, and glory" every day, ten times in the morning and ten times in the evening. Use it when there's a bad situation. Use it when there's a good situation. Either way, things will get better.

Tool: How Much Space Can I Occupy?

Here's another tool you can use when you realize you've put up barriers to being vulnerable. Ask, "How much space can I occupy?" See what's available to you space-wise. Begin by expanding your space out 10 miles in all directions, then 100 miles, then 100,000 miles, and see what it's like. You don't have to feel or see anything, just ask for it to happen and it will.

We have worked with many people who felt that they couldn't be vulnerable, and that they had to put up barriers. When we've asked them to expand their space out 10 miles, then 100 miles, then 100,000 miles in all directions, they have started to laugh because they saw how much energy it takes to keep in place the walls or barriers they have put up, and the way that energy bounces off the walls and ricochets back into their body. It can feel extremely painful.

Have you decided that the only way to handle your discomfort when you are feeling vulnerable is to put up barriers? There is no intimacy when you hide behind barriers.

CHAPTER 5
Gratitude

Gratitude is a state of being grateful or appreciative or thankful.

Mary used to say, "You have to have gratitude. It's not love you want; it's gratitude." She often expressed her gratitude for all the years she had with Bill, and she knew that he was grateful for everything he shared with her, because they freely expressed their appreciation for one another. The caring and the kindness they had with each other was beautiful to behold.

What Is Gratitude?

Gratitude creates a possibility in your life and your relationships that you cannot generate any other way. Gratitude is the act of receiving and acknowledging all things in your life, the good, the bad and the ugly. It is not pretending that everything is perfect. You can still be grateful for things that are not fun, easy or going well.

Gratitude is something you learn. It's not innate. You have to learn to be grateful for what occurs. You can do that by recognizing that whatever happens in your life gives you awareness, and when you are grateful for the awareness you have, it increases your gratitude, which in turn, increases your awareness even more. You may think, "I am feeling grateful for my partner now," or you may notice that you are not feeling any gratitude, but what you may not realize is that feeling grateful is a choice you make moment by moment.

The power of gratitude is that when you are grateful, the Universe contributes to you, so you might want to ask yourself, "How much contribution am I allowing in my life?" And you might want to learn to be grateful for everything that occurs.

Gratitude and Generosity of Spirit

Gratitude and generosity of spirit go hand in hand. Generosity of spirit is the willingness to be happy and grateful for what somebody else has. When you have gratitude and generosity of spirit, everything comes together in your life. People want to do things for you, and you want to do things for them. There is so much ease in everything you do that it doesn't feel like effort. You might not think effort would disappear when you become grateful for what you've got, but it does.

When you are not grateful, you judge that there is a wrongness or a rightness in every choice. Is that judgment real? Is it true? Or is the idea that there is a wrongness or a rightness in every choice you make a lie that limits you? It's a lie that limits you. What if you were grateful for everything that occurred in your life?

True gratitude starts with choosing to be grateful for yourself. You can choose to have gratitude for yourself, for your body, for your partner, for your partner's body, and for everyone and everything in your life, including people who attack you or abuse you.

Why would you be grateful for those people? Because if somebody attacks you or abuses you, what do you know about them? You know they are going to attack or abuse you! You are aware of what they are capable of and what they could do, and then you can choose to act accordingly. And when you are willing to have more awareness, there is much less trauma, drama, upset, and intrigue in your life, and everything will begin to speak to you in a different way.

Designer Gratitude

In this reality, people are trained to say, "Thank you," even when they don't mean it, so they start to think of gratitude as an obligation. They receive something and feel obliged to say, "Thank you." They don't feel any gratitude, they don't even know what gratitude is, but they say, "Thank you." Saying "Thank you" does not equal gratitude.

We call this designer gratitude. It's part of the design of this reality. The designer point of view is about doing the right thing, for the right person, at the right moment, and resenting the hell out of it at the same time. Designer gratitude is the opposite of true gratitude.

Designer gratitude is about what you've *concluded* you are grateful for. That means there's always an *if* or a *because*. "I will be grateful for you *if*..." or "I am grateful for this *because*..." You function as if there's an exchange rate for everything on Earth, so you exchange gratitude or love for what you get. That's very different from the *awareness* of what you're grateful for. Every time you do designer gratitude, you move out of *being* truly grateful and into *doing* gratitude.

You put yourself in a place where you relate to the world from decisions, judgments, conclusions, and computations rather than being the space of infinite possibility, which is beyond relating, beyond relationship, and beyond definition. You can't have the space of *being* without true gratitude, and you can't have true gratitude without the space of *being*.

If you had total gratitude all the time, no one would be able to own you or control you or limit you. No one would be able to make you go into a funk. You'd be like the movie character, Forrest Gump, who was grateful for absolutely everything, no matter what was going on. He said, "My momma always said, 'Life is like a box of chocolates. You never know what you're gonna get.'" And when you're truly grateful for something or someone, you put out an energy that's a celebration.

Gratitude for Yourself and Your Body

You can't begin to have great intimacy with another until you are grateful for yourself and your body. What might that look like? Try watching a cat. A cat loves his body. He does back-flips out of exuberance and runs for the joy of running. When he eats, he eats with relish. He doesn't eat out of obligation or because it's an opportunity to chat with somebody. He won't stop to talk with you in the middle of his dinner. Cats are in total communion with their bodies.

This is not true for most of us. We are mean to our body. We treat our body badly. We judge it, we vilify it, we override it, we drink too much, and we eat too much. None of that is about gratitude. And then we wonder why our body won't do what we want it to do, when we want it to do it, just because we want it done. Be grateful for the fact that your body puts up with you!

What could gratitude for your body look like? A friend of ours once called us from the airport in Dallas, where she and her partner had a ten-hour layover. She said, "We just decided to pay 300 dollars to get a hotel room so we could relax and chill out. I've taken a bath and I'm lying on the bed, and our bodies are so grateful for not having to sit in an airport for ten hours!" Their bodies were grateful that she and her partner were actually listening to them and taking care of them.

Be Grateful for the Body That Is Next to You

You also have to be grateful for the body that's next to you. What if you let go of chasing the fantasy of romantic love and allowed yourself to be totally present with, and grateful for, who your partner is in these ten seconds? Be grateful for who your partner is and for the body that's next to you because it's warm, it's cuddly, it's fuzzy, and it's got parts you can hold onto. Some people do not really care for the body of their partner. They are not enchanted by it. It is something they use for sex, but it's not something they find beautiful. They don't fondly look at it and want to caress it.

This is unfortunate, because if you care for and nurture your partner and your partner's body, they return that caring and nurturing to you. You look at the other person's body and think (regardless of size, shape or health level), "Oh, how beautiful!" and their body begins to react and put forth more sexual energy. But it's not about the return. It's about the gift you receive when you have that point of view. In your gratitude for your partner and his or her body, you expand their reality and yours.

Having Gratitude Is About Building a Muscle

Gratitude is about building a muscle. You build that muscle by going into gratitude for every situation you're in. The more you use the Access Consciousness tools, the greater your capacity for change becomes, and the more gratitude you have. As this happens, you experience a greater sense of ease, and gratitude starts to feel like a natural part of you rather than something requiring effort. You're grateful for having a body. You're grateful for your partner. You're grateful for your life. You're grateful for everything. You're grateful for you! You continue being grateful even when people tell you you're not supposed to be.

Creating Something Greater with Gratitude

Someone once asked us, "Is it possible to have gratitude for everything in my life and to also want things to be different? It seems like a contradiction. How do you operate from gratitude for everything that is, while still wanting more or wanting things to be even better?"

Many of us have been handed the idea that if we're grateful for something, we have to keep it exactly as it is. We think we can only create something greater when we're not grateful for what is or when we hate what is. That is not true. You can have gratitude for something and desire to change it. When you're grateful for everything that shows up in your life, you open up the space to an even greater possibility.

Gratitude was our natural state. We have been taught to not have gratitude for ourselves, our bodies or others. What if your natural state is looking for something greater, and your natural state is also gratitude? You can be totally grateful for what is, and at the same time grateful for the capacity and willingness to ask for and create something greater. You can have the best of all worlds. When you're totally grateful for what is, as it is, you create the space to invite something greater into your life. That's because gratitude gives you a sense of the space of possibility rather than the necessity of a result. Resistance, reaction and judgment create a contraction and shut down the space of what could be created. They never lead to creating something greater. Gratitude, however, opens the space of creation. It allows and invites possibility.

Gratitude is embracing something as it is, *as well as* embracing the capacity you have for being able to create something greater. It's saying, "I'd like that now, please. Thank you very much." When you have gratitude, there is so much possibility and awareness available to you, but you have to be willing to choose it. You have to be willing to have it.

Putting the Tools of Gratitude into Practice

Exercise: Start a Gratitude List

Write down three things about you, your body, your partner, and your life that you're grateful for. Ask:

- What am I grateful for about me?
- What am I grateful for about my body?
- What am I grateful for about my partner and the people in my life?
- What am I grateful for in my life?

We know it sounds corny, and we don't tend to suggest things like this, but try it for a while. Do it for two days. See what happens. Try it for two more days, then three, because, as we've said, gratitude is a choice. When you choose gratitude, you are building a muscle.

Tool: Who Does This Belong To?®

Here's another tool you can use when a judgment comes up. Ask, "Who does this belong to?" If the judgment lightens up at all when you ask that question, know that it is not yours in the first place. It's someone else's judgment.

You don't need to find out whose judgment it is. You don't have to figure out where it came from. You only need to become aware that the judgment isn't yours, and then say, "Return to sender." Send it back to wherever it came from, or else you'll be trying to solve an issue that isn't yours in the first place.

Question:

If I were being grateful today and if I were expressing the gratitude I am and have, how would I be today? What would that look like? What would I choose?

CHAPTER 6

Intimacy with you

Everything we have spoken about so far—honor, trust, allowance, vulnerability, and gratitude—has been about your relationships with others. Your partner. Your family. Your friends. Your lovers. Perhaps even your enemies. However, a question you must ask first is, "Am I willing to have all five of these elements with myself?" Most people are not.

You Are the Constant

Every relationship you will ever have includes one constant presence, you. You bring yourself into every interaction, every conversation, every moment of intimacy. If you do not create intimacy with yourself first, you will always look for external validation of your intimacy.

- When you do not honor yourself, you will look for someone else to do it for you.

- When you do not trust yourself, you will either hand your power to another or refuse to trust anyone at all.
- When you do not allow yourself to be you, you will attempt to control others so they match your points of view.
- When you are not vulnerable with yourself, you will never truly be able to be vulnerable with another.
- When you have no gratitude for yourself, you will constantly need validation, appreciation, or proof from the outside.

Relationships do not fix what you are unwilling to acknowledge within yourself. They amplify it. Let's look at how each element functions within ourselves, because without that internal relationship, intimacy with others becomes transactional or a false performance, rather than expansive, alive, real and generative.

Honor: Are You Willing to Honor You?

Honor is not about liking yourself all the time. It is not about agreeing with everything you do. And it is not about pretending you are "better" than you think you are. Honor is about recognizing what is true for you and not judging or making it wrong.

Most people have been trained to dishonor themselves from a very young age. You were told what was appropriate. What was too much? What was not enough? Little by little, you learned to override what you knew in order to be accepted, loved, safe or fit in.

When you do not honor yourself, you teach others how to dishonor you. What if honor with yourself began with a simple willingness to listen?

- What do you know, even when it doesn't make sense?
- What are you asking for, even when you've been told you shouldn't?
- What would be different if you stopped treating your awareness as false?

Honoring yourself is choosing to not abandon yourself to maintain connection. It is choosing to stay present with what is true for you, even when it's uncomfortable, inconvenient, or different from others.

When you honor yourself, you stop asking relationships to fill the gap where your self-knowing should be.

Trust: Do You Trust You?

True trust with yourself begins with trusting your awareness.

- **Do you trust what you perceive?**
- **Do you trust what your body knows?**
- **Do you trust yourself to know when something is light or heavy, expansive or contractive?**

Most people don't. They invalidate what they know, waving it off as coincidence or just being crazy. They will also often blame others when the outcome reflects the information they refused to acknowledge. Self-trust is not about always choosing correctly according to some moral or societal standard. It is about acknowledging what is true for you in any given moment and being willing to act from that awareness.

When you don't trust yourself, you will either ask others to make decisions for you or refuse to receive input from anyone at all. Neither creates intimacy.

Trust with yourself is what allows you to say, "I made that choice. Now I will choose again." Without self-judgment. Without self-betrayal. Self-trust is also not trying to make your choice right or wrong. Just acknowledging that you made a choice and that you have the ability to choose again.

When you trust yourself, you stop needing guarantees from others. That puts a lot less pressure on relationships if you aren't needing them to validate you.

Allowance: Will You Allow You to Be You?

Allowance means not judging something, even you, for being what it is. Most people are relentlessly unkind to themselves. They judge their thoughts, their bodies, their emotions, their desires, their perceived limitations, and their capacities. We are told to use judgment of ourselves as motivation. That is not motivation. That is abuse. That is abuse of self.

Allowance with yourself is allowing you to have days when you don't know, moments when you wobble, and choices that don't match who you were yesterday. In your life, you will make choices that might not be in your greatest interest but with allowance you don't judge it, you acknowledge the choice, learn from it and with clarity make a new choice. What if you allowed yourself to change without judgment or fear?

When you don't allow yourself to be who you are, you will either try to mold yourself into who others need or told you to be—or demand that others never change so you feel secure. No one is free in that scenario. Allowance with yourself is the foundation of freedom and intimacy in a relationship.

When you allow you, without judgment, to be the brilliant mess that you are, you stop asking others to handle parts of you that you refuse to meet with kindness.

Vulnerability: Are You Willing to Be Honest With You?

Vulnerability is not weakness. It is not telling everyone everything. It is not self-sacrifice. It is not saying mean things to yourself to "motivate" yourself. Vulnerability is the willingness to have no barriers...to anything. Starting with yourself first.

Most people are far more honest with strangers than they are with themselves. They hide their fears, their desires, their sadness, and their anger behind stories of being "fine" or "strong" or "logical." But vulnerability with others requires vulnerability with you.

- **Can you acknowledge when you are hurt without making yourself wrong?**
- **Can you admit when you want something without shaming yourself for wanting it, or making reasons for why you should or shouldn't want it?**
- **Can you be present with your reactions without justifying or suppressing them?**

If you are unwilling to be truly vulnerable with yourself, you will demand emotional transparency from others while withholding your own, shut down intimacy altogether for fear of being exposed, or be your harshest critic. Vulnerability with yourself allows you to see your warts and all and have no judgment of it. You might even enjoy your warts. Vulnerability with yourself combined with allowance and no judgment is what enables true growth, true clarity and the ability to change anything in your life that you may choose.

Vulnerability with yourself creates internal intimacy. That intimacy is what allows connection with others to feel secure, real, and nurturing, rather than tense, dramatic, or unstable.

Gratitude: Are You Grateful for You?

This is often the most confronting element when looking at yourself. Gratitude for yourself has nothing to do with ego, arrogance, separation or superiority. It has everything to do with acknowledging yourself as a contribution.

Most people reserve gratitude for performance. "I'll be grateful for myself when I do better. When I'm more healed. When I get it right. When I have earned it." That is designer gratitude applied internally.

True gratitude for yourself is being grateful that you are here. Grateful that you perceive, that you care (for yourself and others), that you choose, that you keep going, and keep choosing. Gratitude is not given when earned, it is not transactional. Gratitude is one of the most potent energies we have.

- **Are you grateful for your body even when it's not perfect?**
- **Are you grateful for your capacity or desire to change?**
- **Are you grateful for your willingness to ask questions?**

Being grateful for yourself is not selfish or thinking you are better than another, it is knowing you have value. Having gratitude for the brilliance you are, allows you to see and be grateful for the brilliance in others. When you are grateful for you, you no longer need others to prove your worth, and relationships become a choice, not a requirement.

Why This Comes First

Here is the part many people don't like to hear: If you do not have these five elements with yourself, you will unconsciously demand them from others. You cannot create true intimacy with another this way.

That demand shows up as expectations, disappointment, control, withdrawal, judgment, anger or resentment. None of those are intimacy.

When you have honor, trust, allowance, vulnerability, and gratitude with yourself, relationships become generative and nurturing instead of reactive and transactional.

You are no longer asking, "Will you give me what I won't give or have for myself?" You are asking, "What could we create together?"

That is intimacy.

CHAPTER 7

The Five Elements in Daily Life

This book is not an instruction manual for getting relationships "right." You are not meant to finish these pages and suddenly have perfect intimacy with yourself, your partner, your family, or the world. That would simply create another standard to measure yourself against and another place to decide you have failed.

The five elements are not ideals. They are living practices. They show up in ordinary moments, in conversations, in disagreements, in choices made quietly and repeatedly. Each time you choose honor, trust, allowance, vulnerability, or gratitude, something shifts. Not because you fixed yourself or changed anyone else but because you showed up as you. A you that is always striving for more.

You don't need to have these elements "perfect" to create intimacy. Intimacy is not static. It is alive. True intimacy is a living, breathing creation that is changed and enhanced by every choice you and the people in your life make.

What If This Is Where Intimacy Begins?

What if intimacy was a way you lived—a way of being?

What if it showed up not only in romantic relationships, but in friendships, families, workplaces, how you be with yourself and the way you move through the world? What if intimacy was less about closeness and more about presence?

When you choose these elements, you no longer relate from common judgments, expectations, or control. You meet people where they are, you allow difference, you trust awareness over hope. You honor yourself and others without needing agreement. You become willing to be seen, to see and not judge.

You don't have to get this right; you only have to keep choosing.

When honor, trust, allowance, vulnerability, and gratitude become the space you function from, intimacy stops being something you try to create and starts being something that naturally exists.

And from there…everything becomes possible.

www.ingramcontent.com/pod-product-compliance
Lightning Source LLC
LaVergne TN
LVHW091012080826
845145LV00003B/1245

* 9 7 8 1 6 3 4 9 3 7 6 1 0 *